# Play Piano with...

# Mika, Coldplay, Leona Lewis & Other Artists

**Wise Publications**
*part of The Music Sales Group*

London / New York / Paris / Sydney / Copenhagen / Berlin / Madrid / Tokyo

Published by
**Wise Publications**
14-15 Berners Street,
London W1T 3LJ, UK.

Exclusive Distributors:
**Music Sales Limited**
Distribution Centre, Newmarket Road,
Bury St Edmunds, Suffolk IP33 3YB, UK.
**Music Sales Pty Limited**
20 Resolution Drive,
Caringbah, NSW 2229, Australia.

Order No. AM995302
ISBN: 978-1-84772-721-3


Compiled by Nick Crispin.
Edited by Fiona Bolton.
Backing tracks by Paul Honey.
Guitars by Arthur Dick.
CD mixed and mastered by Jonas Persson.

Printed in the EU

**www.musicsales.com**

# Apologize

Words & Music by Ryan Tedder

Demonstration track: Track 1
Backing track only: Track 9
No count in

♩ = 122

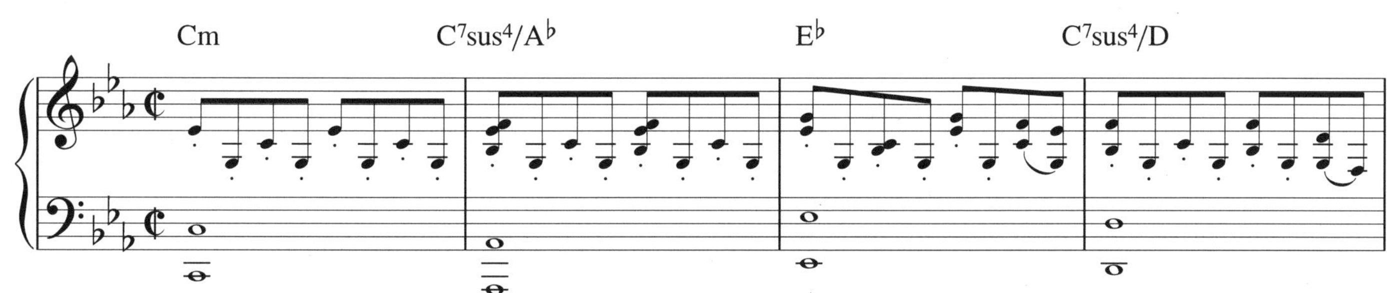


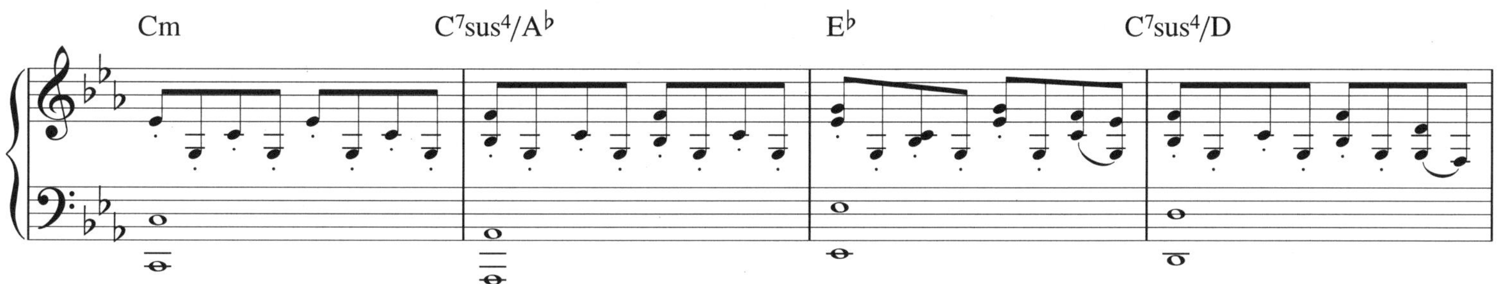


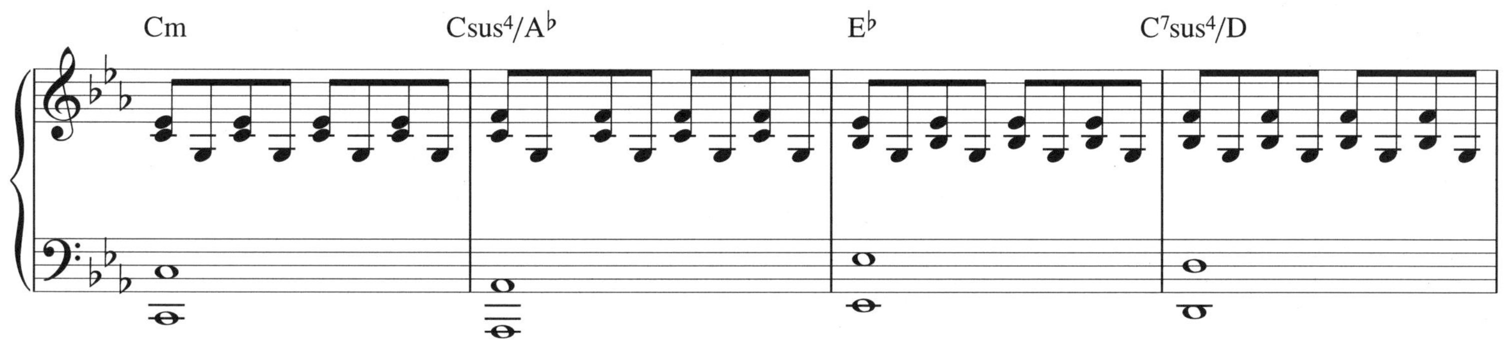


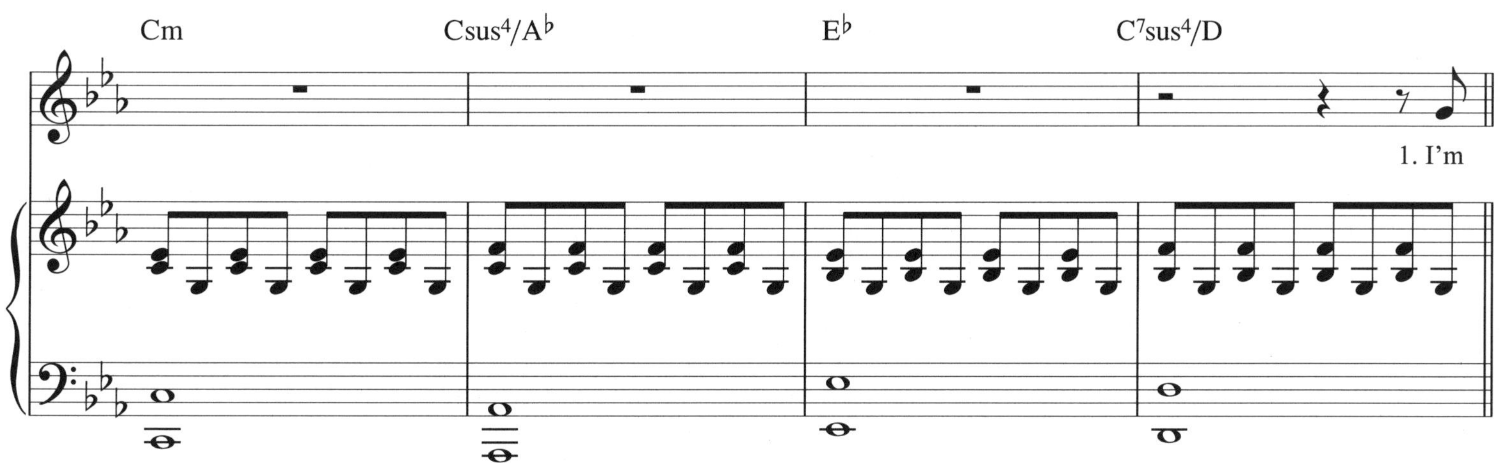

Cm
Csus4/A♭
E♭
hold - ing on your rope, got me ten feet off the ground.
(2.) take an - oth - er chance, take a fall, take a shot for you.

C7sus4/D
Cm
Csus4/A♭
And I'm hear - ing what you say, but I just can't make a sound.
Oh, and I need you like a heart needs a beat, but it's noth - in' new.

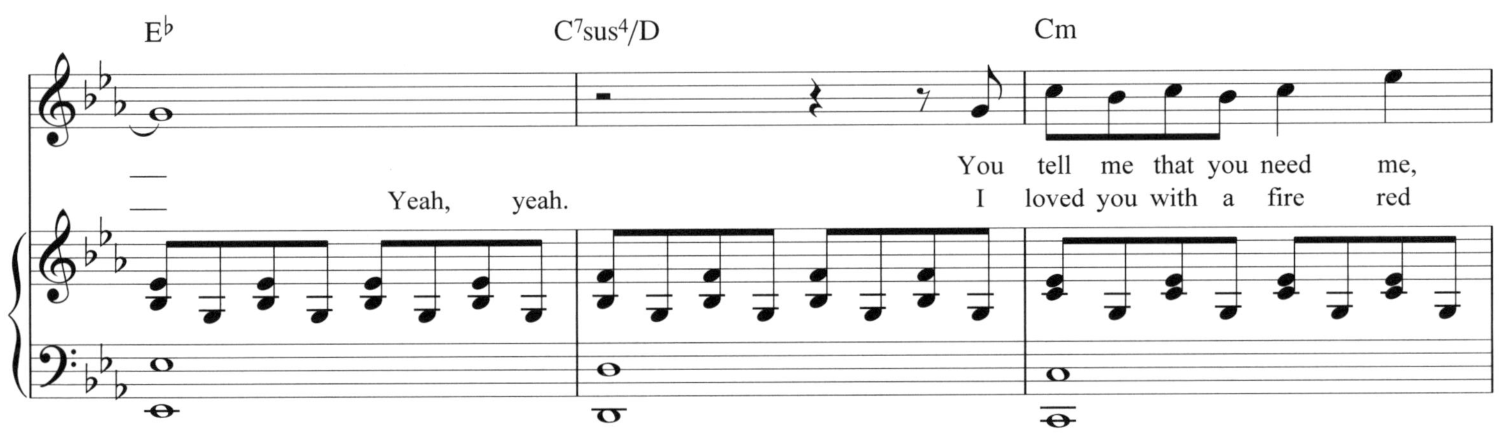
E♭
C7sus4/D
Cm
Yeah, yeah.
You tell me that you need me,
I loved you with a fire red

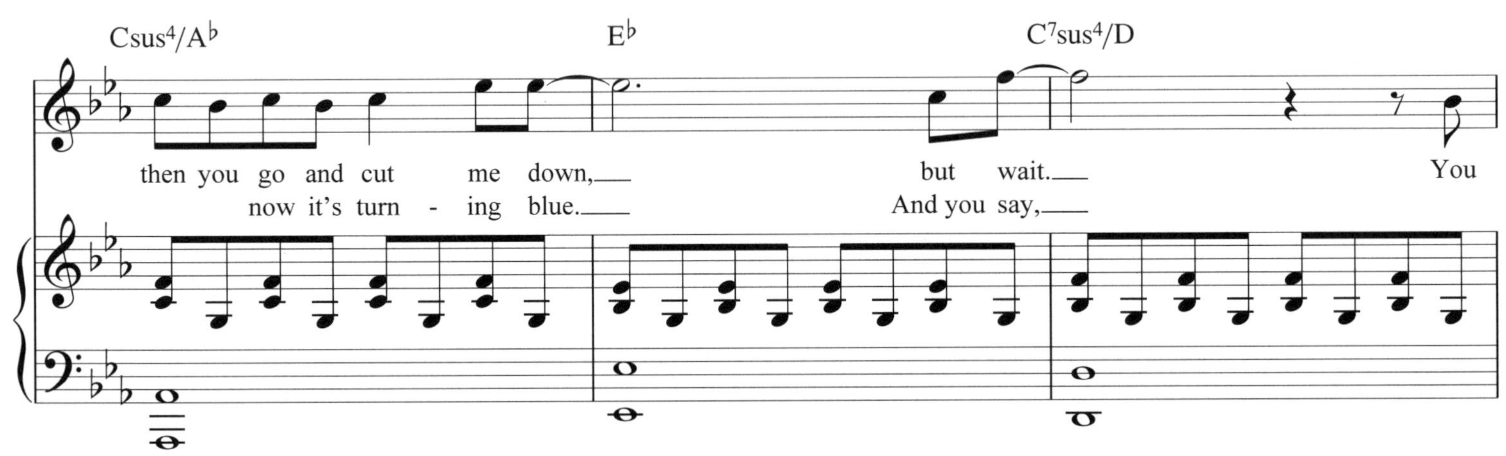
Csus4/A♭
E♭
C7sus4/D
then you go and cut me down, but wait. You
now it's turn - ing blue. And you say,

Cm
Csus4/A♭
E♭
tell me that you're sor - ry, did-n't think I'd turn a - round and say.
sor - ry like an an - gel heav-en let me think was you, but I'm a - fraid.
C7sus4/D
Cm7
That it's too late to a - pol - o - gize.
(1° only)
C7sus4/A♭
E♭
C7sus4/D
It's too late. I said, it's
Cm7
C7sus4/A♭
E♭
C7sus4/D
too late to a-pol-o-gize. It's too late. Too late.

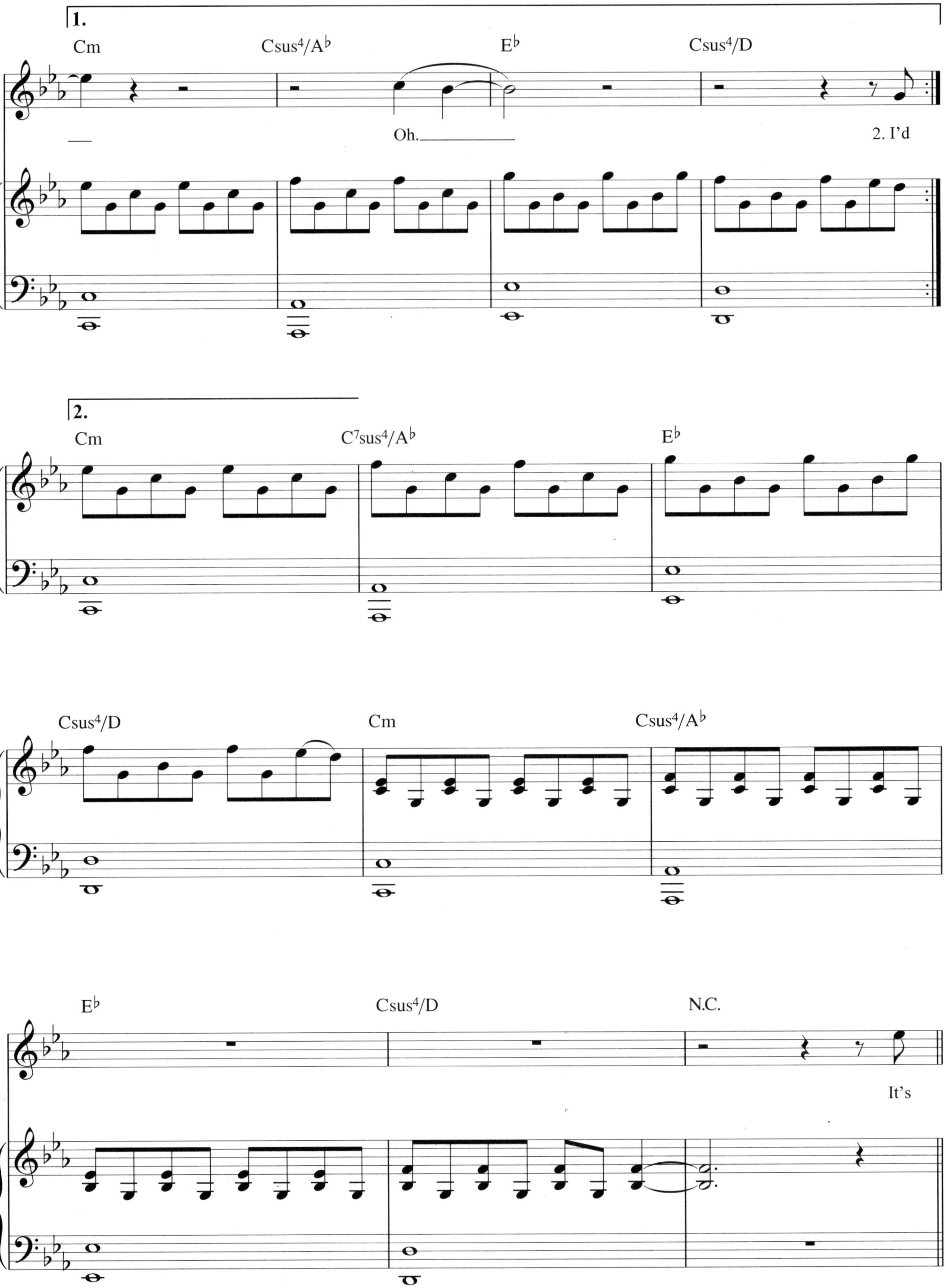

1.

Cm Csus4/A♭ E♭ Csus4/D

— Oh.________ 2. I'd

2.

Cm C7sus4/A♭ E♭

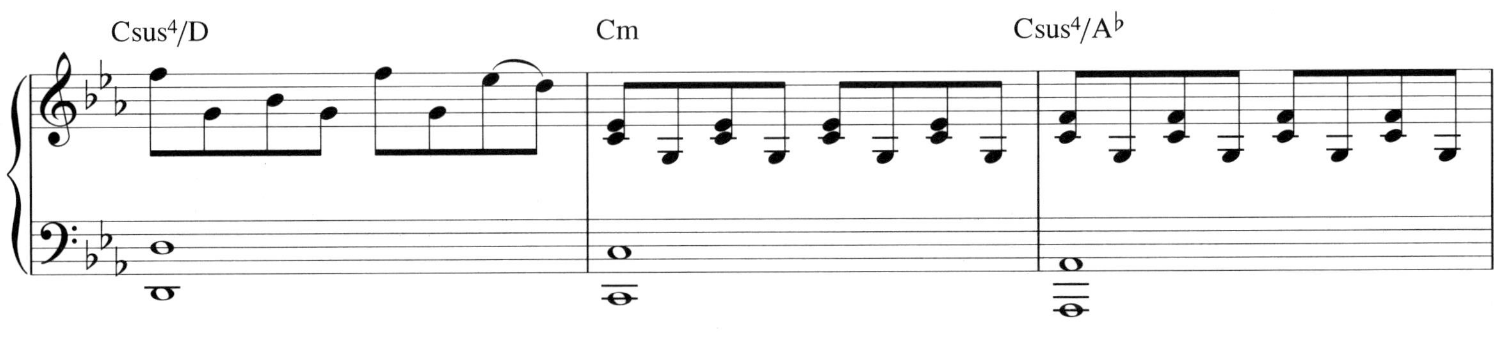

Cm7
C7sus4/A♭
E♭
too late to a - pol - o - gize.
It's too late.
C7sus4/D
Cm7
C7sus4/A♭
I said, it's too late to a - pol - o - gize.
It's
1.
2.
E♭
C7sus4/D
C7sus4/D
too late.
I said, it's
I'm
Cm
rall.
Csus4/A♭
E♭
hold - ing on your rope, got me ten feet off the ground.

# Better In Time

Words & Music by Andrea Martin & Jonathan Rotem

Demonstration track: Track 2
Backing track only: Track 10
Count in: 1 bar

E♭m
G♭/D♭
C♭
I did - n't know where to turn to.
with - out some - thing there to re - mind me.
G♭
B♭m
See, some - how I can't for - get you,
Was it all that eas - y
E♭m
G♭/D♭
C♭
af - ter all that we've been through.
to just put a - side your feel - ings?
G♭
B♭m
Go - ing, com - ing, thought I heard a knock. Who's there? No - one. Think - ing that
If I'm dream - ing, don't wan - na laugh. Hurt my feel - ings, but that's the path

E♭m
G♭/D♭
C♭
I de - serve it. Now I re - al - ise that I real - ly did - n't know.
I be - lieve in and I know time will heal it.
If
G♭
B♭m
you did - n't no - tice, you mean ev - 'ry - thing. Quick - ly I'm learn - ing to love a - gain.
E♭m
G♭/D♭
C♭
3
All I know is I'm gon' be O. K.
G♭
B♭m
Thought I could - n't live with - out you. It's gon - na hurt when it heals too.

E♭m
G♭/D♭
3
C♭
Oh, yeah. It - 'll all get bet - ter in time.
G♭
B♭m
And e - ven though I real - ly love you, I'm gon - na smile 'cause I de - serve
E♭m
G♭/D♭
C♭
to. It - 'll all get bet - ter in time.
A♭m7
G♭/B♭
Since there's no more you and me,

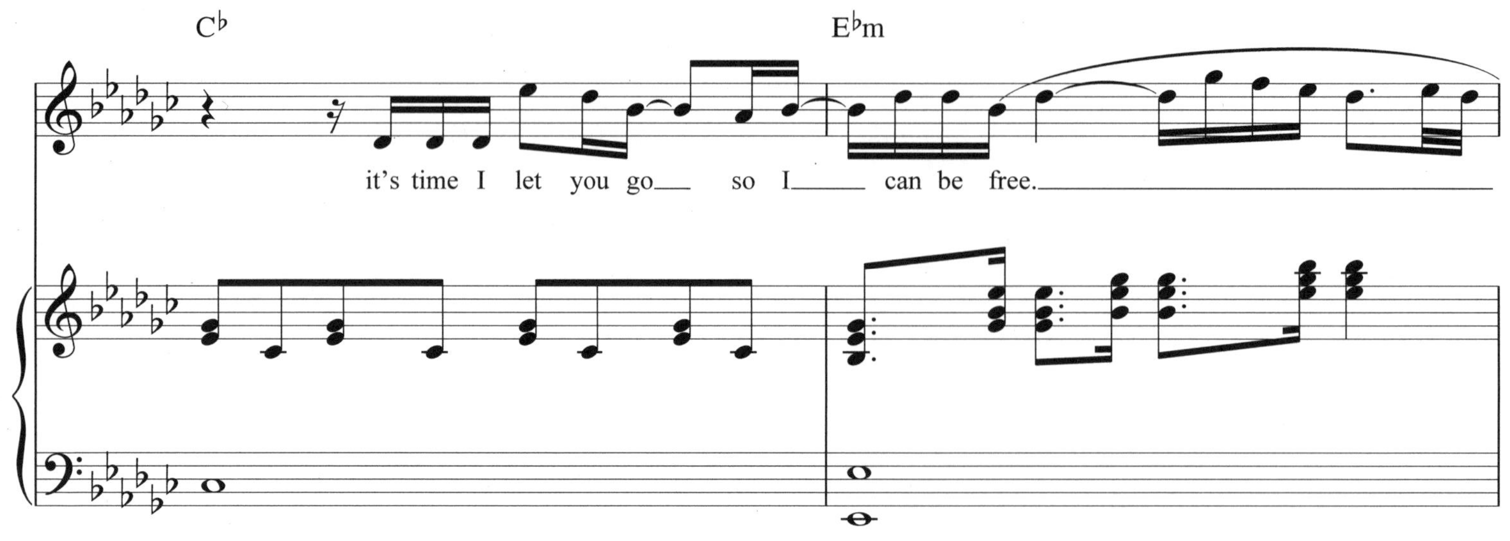
C♭
E♭m
it's time I let you go so I can be free.

A♭m7
G♭/B♭
And live my life how it should be.

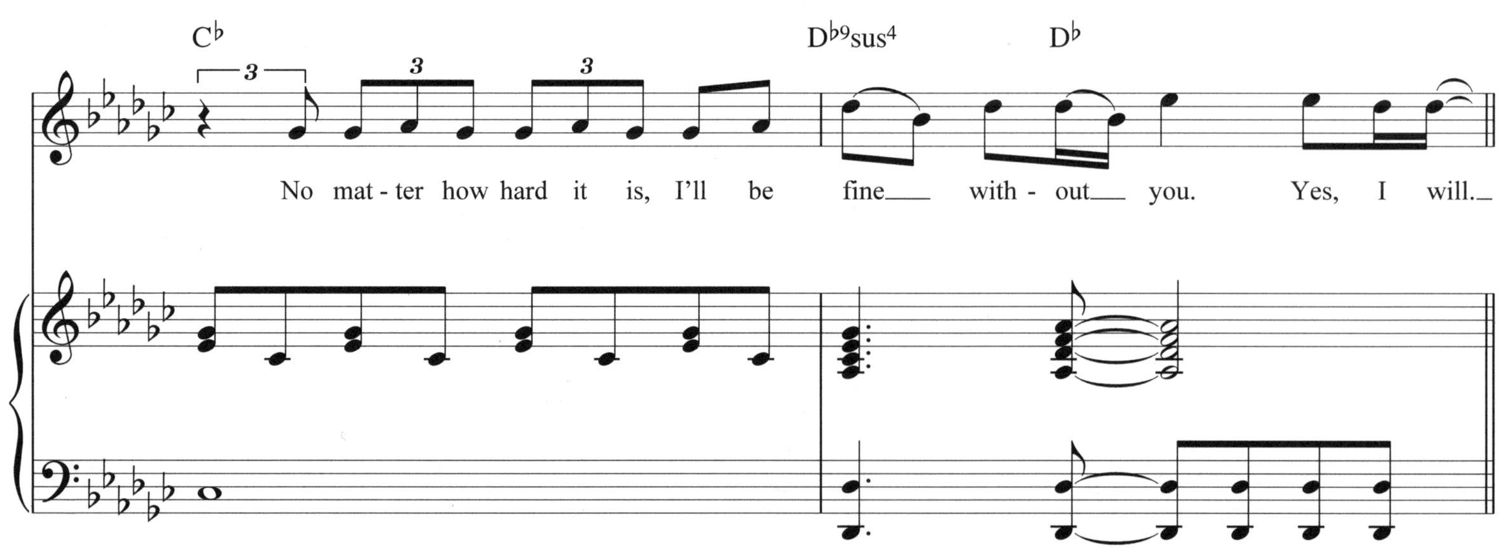
C♭
D♭9sus4
D♭
No mat - ter how hard it is, I'll be fine with - out you. Yes, I will.

G♭
B♭m
Thought I could-n't live with-out you.
It's gon-na hurt when it heals too.
E♭m
G♭/D♭
C♭
3
Oh.
It - 'll all get bet - ter in time.
G♭
B♭m
And e-ven though I real-ly love you,
I'm gon-na smile 'cause I de - serve
E♭m
G♭/D♭
C♭
Repeat and fade
3
to. Yes, I do.
It - 'll all get bet - ter in time.

# Carry You Home

Words & Music by Max Martin & James Blunt

Demonstration track: Track 3
Backing track only: Track 11
No count in

♩ = 83

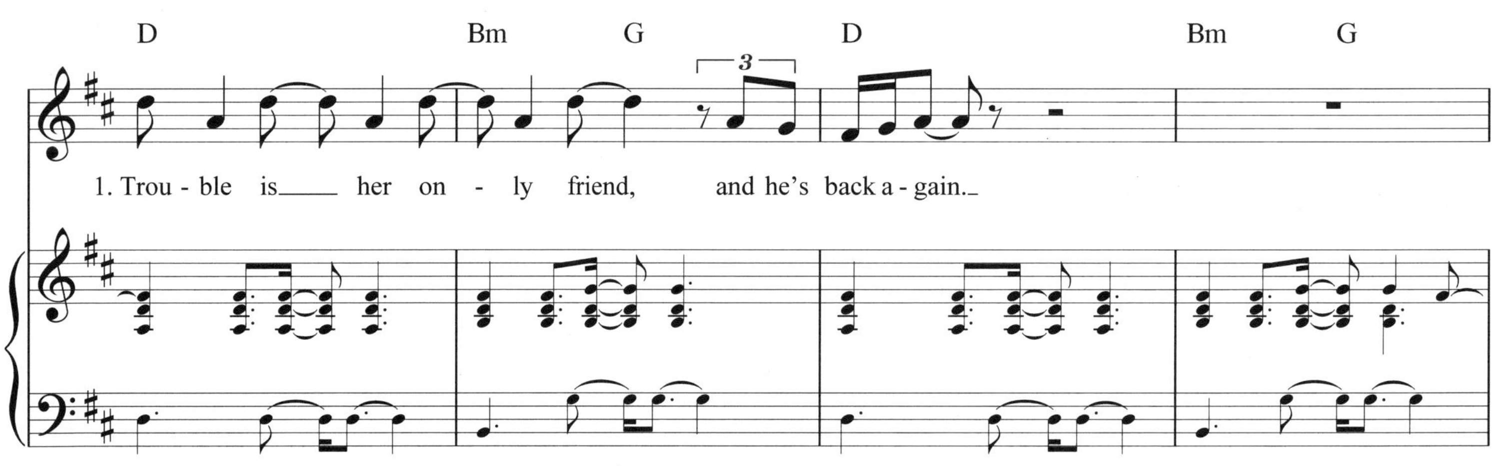


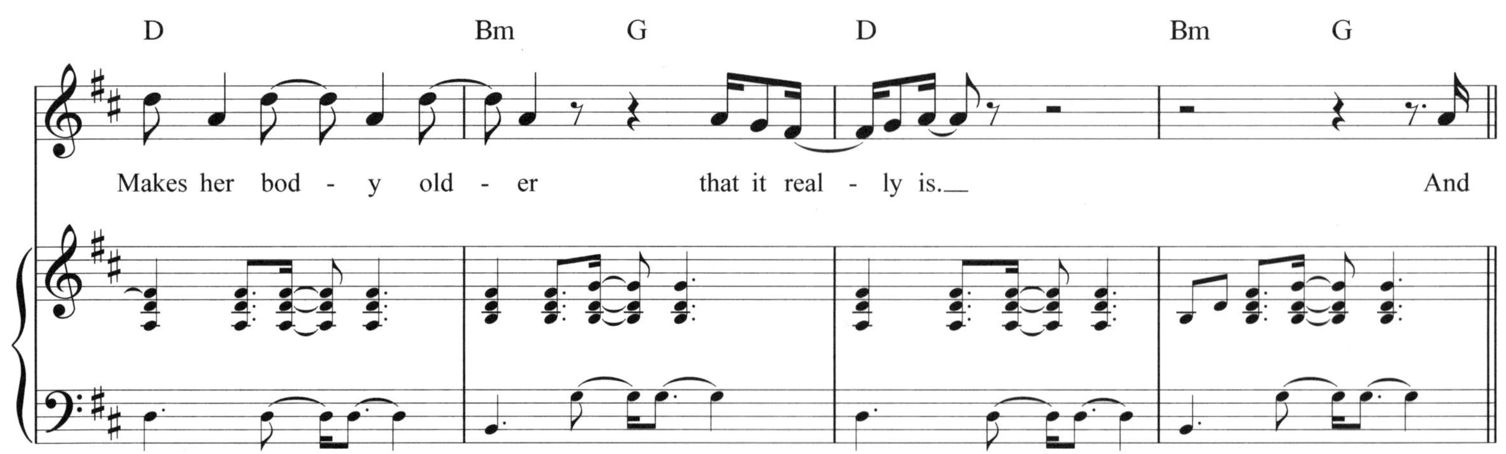

D
Bm
G
she says it's high time she went a - way, no-one's got much to say, in
2. If she had wings she would fly a - way, and an - oth - er day God will give
D
Bm
G
D
this town.
her some.
Trou - ble is the on -
Bm
G
- ly way is down. Down down. As strong as you were,
D
Bm9
F♯m
ten - der you go. I'm watch - ing you breath - ing for the last time.

Gmaj9
D
Bm9
A song for your heart, but when it is quiet, I know what it means
To Coda
1.
F♯m
G
D
and I'll car - ry you home. I'll car - ry you home.
Bm
G
D
Bm
G
2.
D
Em7
D
And they're all born pret - ty in New York Cit - y to - night.

Asus4
Em7
D
And some - one's lit - tle girl was tak - en from the world to - night.
Asus4
Em7
D
A
Un - der the stars and stripes.
D.S. al Coda
Coda
G
G11
As strong as you were,
As strong as you were,
D
Bm7
ten - der you go.
I'm watch - ing you breath -

F♯m7
Gmaj7
D
- ing for the last time. A song for your heart, but when it is qui -
Bm7
F♯m7
Gmaj9
- et, I know what it means and I'll car - ry you home.
D
Bm
G
I'll car - ry you home.
D
Bm
G
D
8vb

# Hurt

Words & Music by Christina Aguilera, Linda Perry & Mark Ronson

Demonstration track: Track 4
Backing track only: Track 12
Count in: 1 bar

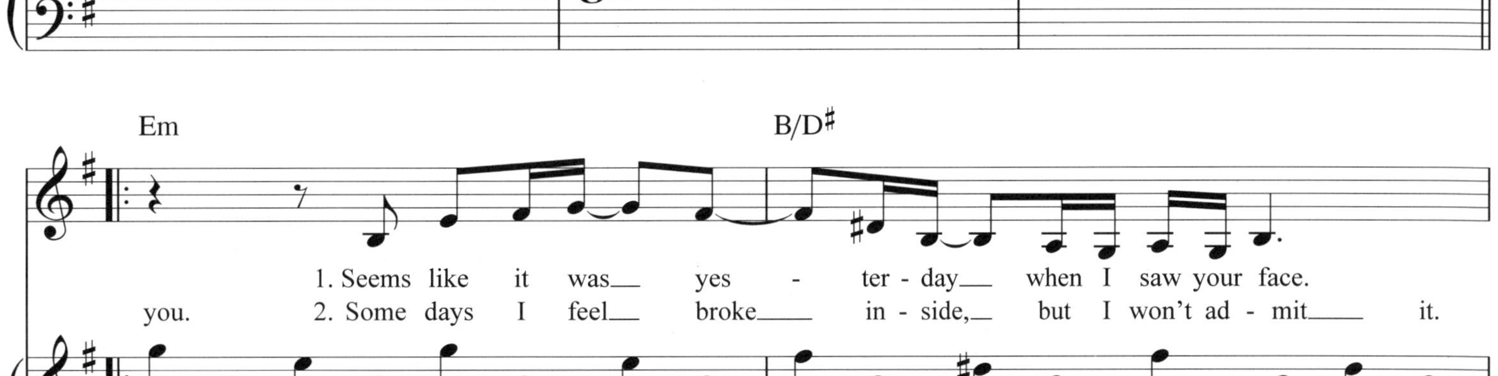

B
If on - ly I knew what I know to - day.
And it's so hard to say good - bye when it comes to this.
Em
Ooh, ooh. I would
Ooh. Would you
*
C
C6
A/C♯
hold you in my arms, I would take the pain a - way;
tell me I was wrong? Would you help me un - der - stand? Are you
D
B7/D♯
thank you for all you've done, for - give all your mis - takes. There's
look - ing down up - on me? Are you proud of who I am? There's

C
C6
A/C♯
noth-ing I would-n't do to hear your voice a-gain. Some
noth-ing I would-n't do to have just one more chance, to
D
B7/D♯
times I wan-na call you, but I know you won't be there.
look in-to your eyes and see you look-ing back.
Em
B/D♯
Em
Whoa, I'm sor-ry for blam-ing you for ev-'ry-thing
C
Em
C6
C/B
Am
1.
B
I just could-n't do; and I've hurt my-self by hurt-ing
3

2.
B
Em
G/D
-self,
oh.
If I had just one more day,
Cmaj7
I would tell you how much that I've missed you since you've been a-
C6
Am
E/G♯
-way.
Oh, it's dan-ger-ous,
it's so out of
C/G
F♯m7♭5
line
to try and turn back

B
Em
time.
I'm sor - ry for
B/D♯
Em
Cmaj7
C6
C
blam - ing you for ev - 'ry - thing I just could-n't do;
poco rit.
a tempo
Am
B
C
and I've hurt my - self...
rit.
a tempo
Am7
B
Em
by hurt - ing you.

# Grace Kelly

Words & Music by Jodi Marr, Dan Warner, John Merchant & Michael Penniman

Demonstration track: Track 5
Backing track only: Track 13
Count in: 1 bar

G
D
I could be whole - some, I could be loath - some, guess I'm a lit - tle bit shy.
G
N.C.
Why don't you like me, why don't you like me with - out mak - ing me try?
G
Dm7
I try to be like Grace Kel - ly
Am7
D7sus4
D7
G
but all her looks were too sad.
So I try a lit - tle

Dm7
Am7
Am7/D
D
Fred - die.
I've gone i - den - ti - ty mad.
G
I could be brown, I could be blue, I could be vi - o - let
C
C/D
D
sky. I could be hurt - ful, I could be pur - ple, I could be an - y - thing you like.
G
Got - ta be green, got - ta be mean, got - ta be ev - 'ry - thing

To Coda I
C
C/D
D
more. Why don't you like me? Why don't you like me? Why don't you walk out the door?
1.
G
Spoken: (Getting angry doesn't solve anything.)
G
How can I help it, how can I help it, how can I help what you
C
C/D
D
think? Hel - lo my ba - by, hel - lo my ba - by, put - ting my life on the

G
brink. Why don't you like me, why don't you like me, why don't you like___ your -
C
- self? Should I bend o - ver, should I look
C/D
old - er just to be
D
put on your__ shelf?_
2.
C
8va
Cm7
Say what you want to sat
G
- is - fy___ your - self._
C
Cm/E♭
But you on - ly want what ev -

G
D/F♯
Em
G/D
C♯m7♭5
-'ry - bod - y else says you should want.
D7sus4♭9
You want.
G
I could be brown, I could be blue, I could be vi - o - let
C
C/D
D
sky. I could be hurt - ful, I could be pur - ple, I could be an - y - thing you like.

G
Got - ta be green, got - ta be mean, got - ta be ev - 'ry - thing
C
more. Why don't you like me? Why don't you
C/D
like me?
D
Walk out the door.
G
I could be brown, I could be blue, I could be vi - o - let
C
sky. I could be hurt - ful, I could be
C/D
pur - ple, I could be
D
an - y - thing you like.

G
Got - ta be green, got - ta be mean, got - ta be ev - 'ry - thing
C
C/D
D
more. Why don't you like me? Why don't you like me? Walk out the door.
Em
D
C
G/B
Ooh.
8va
Am7
G
Fmaj9
(8)

# Love Song

Words & Music by Sara Bareilles

Demonstration track: Track 6
Backing track only: Track 14
Count in: 1 bar

Dm
C/E
F
D/F♯
Gm
F/A
know
that.
You made room for me,
down
un - der
you
and your twist - ed
B♭sus2
C
Dm
C/E
F
D/F♯
3
but it's too soon to see
if I'm hap - py in your hands.
words, your help just hurts.
You are not what I thought you were.
Gm
F/A
B♭sus2
C
Dm
C/E
F
D/F♯
I'm un - us - ual - ly
hard to hold on
to.
Hel - lo
to high
and dry.
Gm
F/A
B♭sus2
Blank stares at blank pag - es.
No eas - y way
Con - vinced me to please you.
Made me think

C D/F♯ Gm F/A
to say this. You mean well, but you make this hard
that I need this too. I'm try - ing to let you hear
B♭sus2 Gm
on me. I'm not gon-na write you a love song 'cause you asked
me as I am.
C7 F/A B♭sus2 D/F♯
for it, 'cause you need one, you see. I'm not gon-na write you a
Gm C7 F/A
love song 'cause you tell me it's make or break - ing this, if you're on

B♭sus2 D/F♯ Gm F/A
3
you way. I'm not gon-na write you to stay. If
Dm G/B B♭sus2
all you have is leav-ing, I'm gon' need a bet-ter rea-son to write you a love
1.
C Gm F/A B♭sus2 C
song to-day. To-day.
2.
Dm C/E F D/F♯ Gm
'Cause you asked

C7
F/A
B♭sus2
for it, 'cause you need one, you see. I'm not gon-na write you a
1.
Gm
C7
F/A
love song 'cause you tell me it's make or break - ing this. Is
2.
B♭sus2
D/F♯
Gm
F/A
that why you want-ed a love song? 'Cause you asked - ing this, if you're on
B♭sus2
D/F♯
Gm
F/A
B♭
your way. I'm not gon-na write you to stay. If your heart is no-where in it, I don't

C
Dm
G7/B
want it for a min - ute. Babe, I'll walk the sev- en seas when I be - lieve that there's a rea - son to write
B♭
C
Gm
F/A
you a love song to - day.
B♭sus2
C
Dm
C/E
F
D/F♯
3
To - day.
Gm
F/A
B♭sus2
C
Dm
C/E
F
8vb

# Take A Bow

Words & Music by Mikkel Eriksen, Tor Erik Hermansen & Shaffer Smith

Demonstration track: Track 7
Backing track only: Track 15
Count in: 1 bar

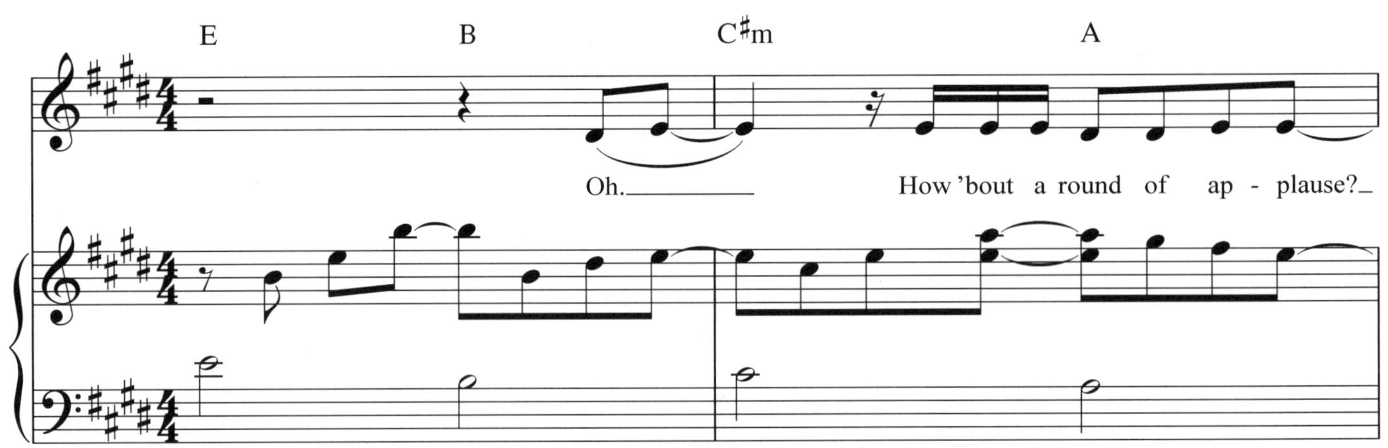

E
B
C#m
A
1. You look so dumb right now,
2. Grab your clothes and get gone,
you'd bet - ter hur - ry up,
E
B
C#m
A
E
B
stand - ing out - side my house.
be - fore the sprink - lers come on.
Try - ing to a - pol - o - gise,
Talk - ing 'bout, "Girl I love you, you're the one."
C#m
A
E
B/D#
Dsus2
you're so ug - ly when you cry.
This just looks like a re - run.
Please! Just cut it out.
Please! What else is on?
And
E
B
C#m
A
Don't tell me you're sor - ry 'cause you're not.
Ba - by, when I

E
B
D
know you're on - ly sor - ry you got caught.
But you
E
B
C♯m7
Asus2
E
B
put on quite a show,
real - ly had me go - ing,
but now it's time to go,
C♯m7
Asus2
E
B
C♯m7
Asus2
cur-tain's fin - al - ly clos - ing.
That was quite a show,
ver - y en - ter - tain - ing,
F♯m7
E/G♯
A
E/G♯
D
To Coda
but it's o - ver now.
Go on and take a bow.
Oh.

B/A
B
C♯m7
F♯m7
E/G♯
And the a - ward for the best lie goes to you for mak-ing me
B/A
B
C♯m7
D
be - lieve that you could be faith-ful to me. Let's hear your speech. Oh.
E
B
C♯m
A
E
B
How 'bout a round of ap - plause?
Stand-ing o - va -
Dsus2
D.S. al Coda
- tion?
But you
Coda
rit.
F♯m7
E/G♯
A
But it's o - ver now.

# Violet Hill

Words & Music by Guy Berryman, Chris Martin, Jon Buckland & Will Champion

Demonstration track: Track 8
Backing track only: Track 16
Count in: 1 bar

A
Asus4/2
F♯m
froze down be - low. When the fu -
cross was held a - loft. Bur-
A
Aadd4
Badd9
- ture's ar - chi - tec - tured by a car - ni - val of id - i - ots on
- y me in ar - mour, when I'm dead and hit the ground, my nerves are
C♯m
Badd9
G♯m
A
G♯m
E
show, you'd bet - ter lie low. If you love me, won't you
poles that un - froze. And if you love me, won't you
C♯m
B6
C♯m
1.
2.
let me know?
let me know?
2. Was a long
Guitar

C♯m
C♯m9
A
Asus4/2
1.
2.
F♯m
F♯m
A
Aadd4
I don't wan - na be a sol - dier who a cap-
Badd9
C♯m
Badd9
G♯m
- tain of some sink-ing ship would stow far be - low. So, if you
A
G♯m
E
C♯m
B6
C♯m
love me, why'd you let me go?

2 3 4 5 6 7 8 9
5/09 (169674)

# CD Track Listing

Full performance demonstration tracks...

## 1. Apologize
(Tedder)
Sony/ATV Music Publishing (UK) Limited.

## 2. Better In Time
(Martin/Rotem)
Sony/ATV Music Publishing (UK) Limited)/IQ Music Limited.

## 3. Carry You Home
(Martin/Blunt)
EMI Music Publishing Limited/Kobalt Music Publishing Limited.

## 4. Hurt
(Aguilera/Perry/Ronson)
Sony/ATV Music Publishing (UK) Limited/EMI Music Publishing Limited/
Universal Music Publishing MGB Limited.

## 5. Grace Kelly
(Marr/Warner/Merchant/Penniman)
Universal Music Publishing Limited/Sony/ATV Music Publishing (UK) Limited/
Sony/ATV Harmony (UK) Limited.

## 6. Love Song
(Bareilles)
Sony/ATV Music Publishing (UK) Limited.

## 7. Take A Bow
(Eriksen/Hermansen/Smith)
Imagem Music Limited/Sony/ATV Music Publishing (UK) Limited/
EMI Music Publishing Limited.

## 8. Violet Hill
(Berryman/Martin/Buckland/Champion)
Universal Music Publishing MGB Limited.

Backing tracks only (without piano)...

## 9. Apologize

## 10. Better In Time

## 11. Carry You Home

## 12. Hurt

## 13. Grace Kelly

## 14. Love Song

## 15. Take A Bow

## 16. Violet Hill

To remove your CD from the plastic sleeve, lift the small lip to break the perforations.
Replace the disc after use for convenient storage.